CZERNY *for* GUITAR

12 SCALE STUDIES FOR CLASSICAL GUITAR

Etudes Based on *School of Velocity, Op. 299*

Cover photo by Christopher Peters

ISBN 978-1-4234-8512-4

HAL•LEONARD®
CORPORATION

7777 W. BLUEMOUND RD. P.O. BOX 13819 MILWAUKEE, WI 53213

In Australia Contact:
Hal Leonard Australia Pty. Ltd.
4 Lentara Court
Cheltenham, Victoria, 3192 Australia
Email: ausadmin@halleonard.com.au

Visit Hal Leonard Online at
www.halleonard.com

INTRODUCTION

Practicing studies (etudes) as a part of any technical routine is vital to a musician's development. While it is important to practice exercises and scales alone, studies challenge us to focus on particular aspects of technique in the context of a musical composition.

Over the years I have collected a good number of wonderful studies for the left and right hands that I continually rotate into my practice routine. However, when it comes to scales, I have always been a little dissatisfied with the guitar study repertoire. In my frustration, I have been compelled to seek a solution in the repertoire of other instruments. I found a perfect example of what I was looking for in Carl Czerny's *School of Velocity, Op. 299* for piano. The study I chose to arrange initially addresses both ascending and descending scales of varying lengths, repeated patterns, large intervallic leaps, and transitions from chords to scales. In addition, it represents a wide tonal range, which, on the guitar, translates to a thorough exploration of the fingerboard vertically and horizontally.

Sometimes technique is characterized too narrowly as, "Fast and clean playing equals good technique." As a result, many tend to practice with only those goals in mind. And while speed and accuracy are worthy aspirations, they only represent a few limited aspects of technique and are by no means the sole determining factors as to how accomplished or advanced a musician is. I prefer to think of technique as encompassing everything a musician does physically to play his instrument. Technique is a means to an end—that end being musical expression, creativity, and interpretation.

The practice of scales presents the musician with vast possibilities for development of hands, ears, eyes, and mind. It is with this intention that I have arranged the first of the Czerny studies in Op. 299 in twelve keys with twelve different approaches or "treatments." You will explore a variety of articulations, ranges, and technical perspectives as you learn each key. Therefore, these arrangements will not only improve your ability to play scales fluently, but will also develop your fingerboard knowledge, ears, reading ability, as well as strength and endurance. The order of the studies is based on difficulty and technical approach rather than key. I hope these arrangements will contribute to your technical and musical development and that you will enjoy working on them as much as I have!

David Patterson

STUDY 1: B♭ Major

Playing at a continuous, relaxed velocity is a great way to warm up your fingers and get them in sync while building endurance and control. At one point, I had the privilege of studying electric guitar with Joe Stump—one of the best heavy metal shredder guitarists on the planet—and he referred to this as "relaxed but aerobic" playing. He viewed it much in the same way as one might view jogging on a treadmill to warm up before beginning a workout. Of course for Joe, a relaxed aerobic tempo was sixteenth notes at 180 BPM! However, you won't need to get anywhere near that kind of speed in order to enjoy the full benefits of this study.

Rest assured, regardless of what your individual pace is, this study will get your fingers moving together as well as develop your ability to play evenly and fluidly. The first thing here is to learn the notes carefully. Begin slowly enough to get through the study without mistakes, so that your fingers learn the patterns automatically. It's pretty straight forward, but there are a few curveballs in there, so never play any faster than you can anticipate the little twists and turns.

Once you start to feel as though you have the notes under your fingers, begin using a metronome to keep a steady tempo. Concentrate primarily on playing legato and evenly with good tone. Find a tempo where your fingers flow comfortably. Increased speed will be a byproduct and will come naturally over time, so be patient and don't get obsessed with constantly pushing the tempo. If you are missing notes, playing unevenly, unable to control tone, tensing up, or feeling discomfort in your hands, slow down!

PRACTICE TIPS:

- One of the great benefits of this arrangement is that, because it uses no open strings, it can be transposed easily into many keys. Try it in multiple positions. It will feel quite different depending on where you play it on the fingerboard.
- Come up with several dynamic schemes. Practice crescendos and decrescendos over varying lengths. Working dynamics into scale practice is very valuable.
- Try alternately accenting different fingers through the entire study. This is great practice for control and finger awareness.
- Breathe! You should be breathing naturally as you play. This applies to all playing, by the way. Holding your breath is a sure sign of tension.

AN AEROBIC WORKOUT

C. Czerny
arr. David Patterson

V pos.

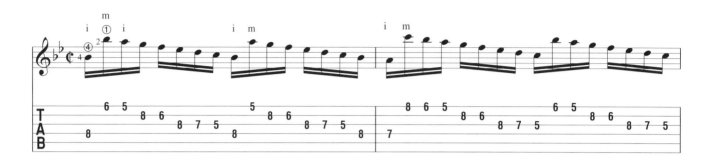

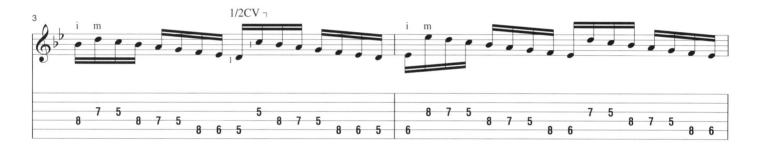

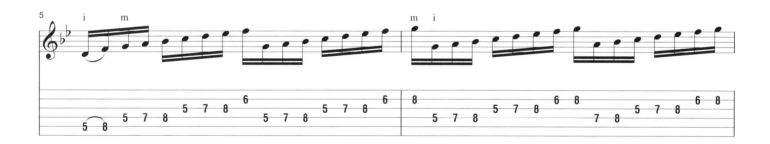

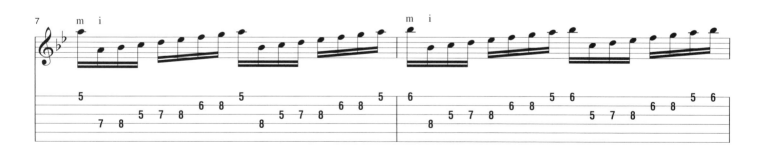

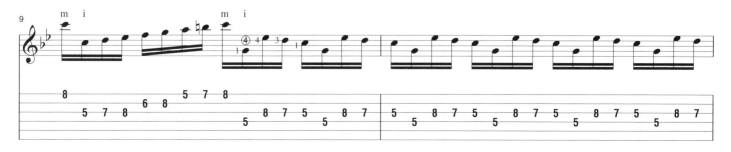

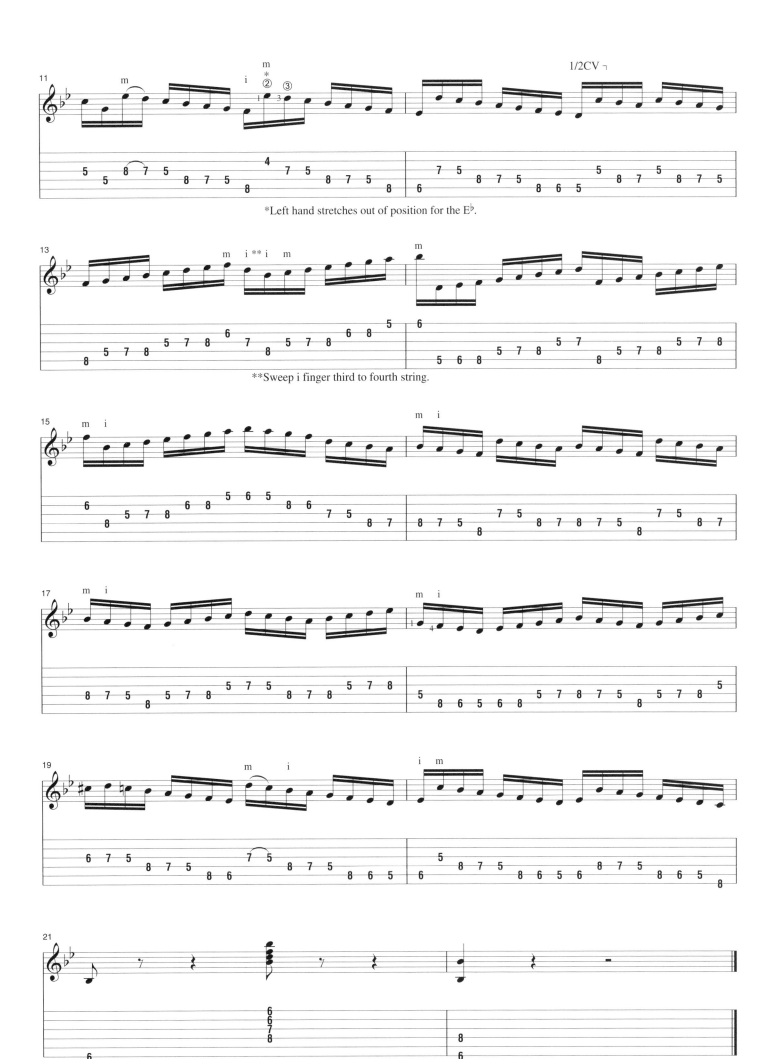

*Left hand stretches out of position for the E♭.

**Sweep i finger third to fourth string.

STUDY 2: F Major

Practicing 3rds is another great "aerobic workout" for both hands. You get to play a lot of notes, work on string crossing in the right hand, and improve synchronization while practicing a very common sequence. The 5/4 time accommodates the pattern while offering an opportunity to practice playing in an odd time signature. If you have a programmable metronome or drum machine, try creating beat patterns in 2+3 and 3+2 to the quarter note so you can experience different accent patterns within the measure.

PRACTICE TIPS:

- Try some different things like dotted rhythms and speed bursts.

- I use an open string sometimes to transition to another position. Work to match the tone and sustain of that note with the closed notes so the passage is seamless.

- Keep your right hand perpendicular to the strings as you cross. Sometimes the right hand will drift toward the bridge or the neck when playing a lot of notes and crossing strings.

- As with many of these studies, use various right-hand combinations including p–i and/or p–m.

SEQUENTIAL 3RDS

C. Czerny
arr. David Patterson

*Right hand finger is repeated to begin new pattern.

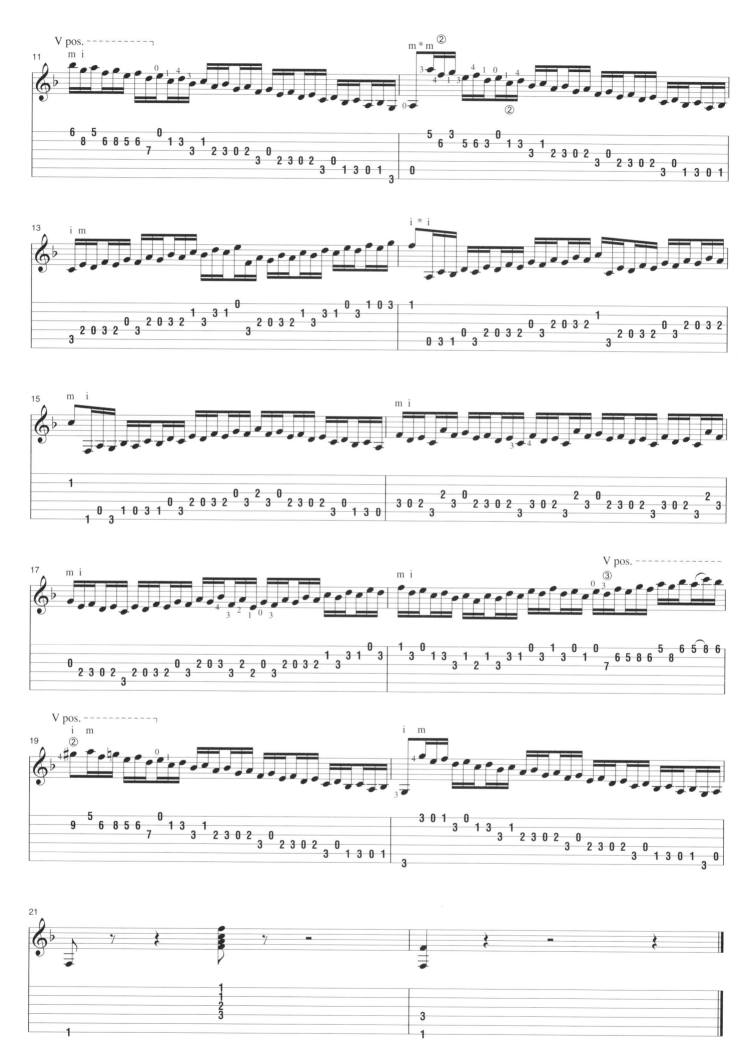

STUDY 3: F♯ Major

Practicing scales with repeated notes in the right hand is great for endurance, coordination, and evenness. This study should be played rest-stroke and free-stroke using various right-hand combinations (m–a/i–a/p–i). When you feel confident with the notes, I highly recommend that you add dynamics to this study. This will challenge you further and hone your right hand control.

PRACTICE TIPS:

- Slow the tempo down and try accenting the second articulation (repeated note). It will be difficult at first but will improve your finger awareness.

- Once you've learned the study with two articulations per pitch, add another note to make it three articulations per pitch.

- This study is another good candidate for using dotted rhythms as a practice tool.

REPEATED NOTES

C. Czerny
arr. David Patterson

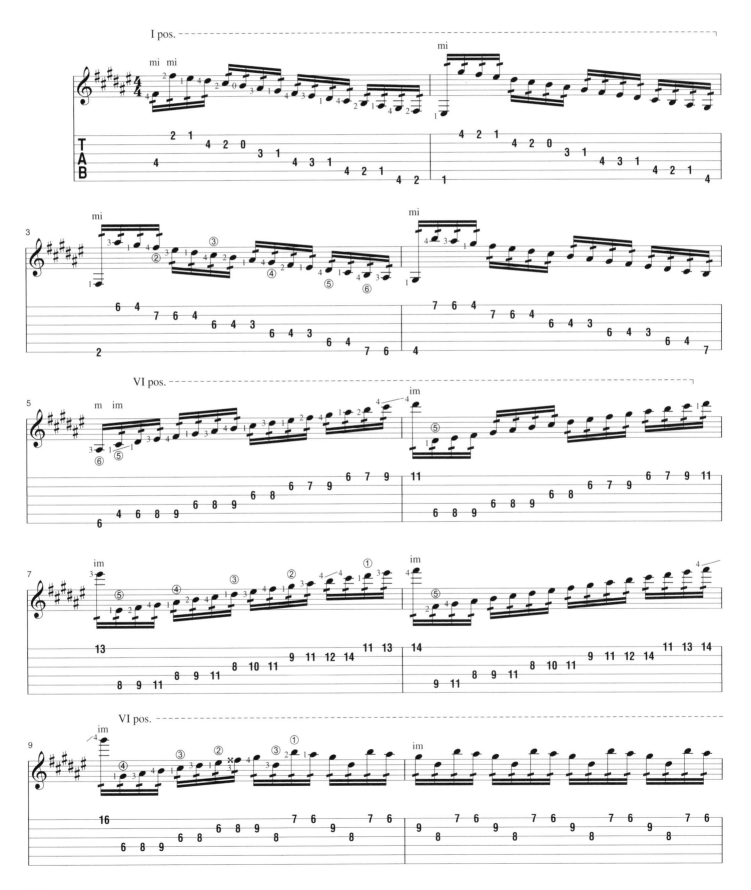

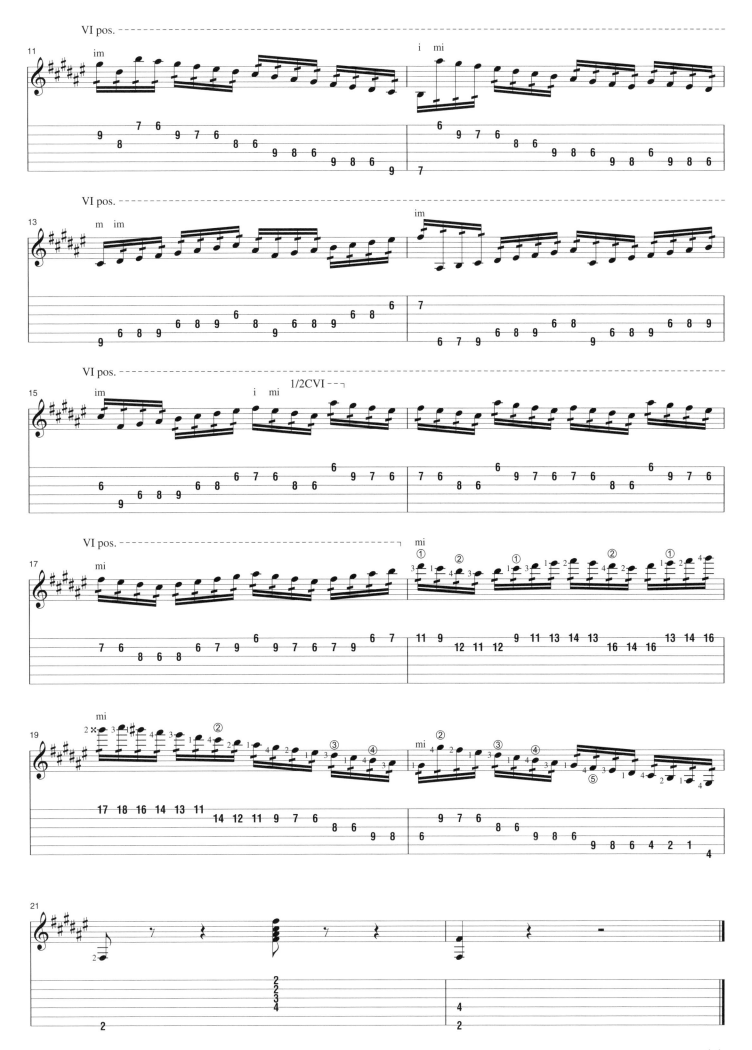

STUDY 4: A Major

Slurs are a major part of every guitarist's technique, and mastering the basic two-note slur is good place to start. In this study, you will be playing both ascending slurs (hammer-ons) and descending slurs (pull-offs).

PRACTICE TIPS:

- When hammering strings, be sure to relax the pressure after the snap. Don't continue to press into the string any harder than it takes to sustain the note

- Remember that pull-offs are simply a way to pluck the string. Therefore, many of the same criteria for tone and volume apply: direction of the finger, stiffness of the tip joint etc. Most pull-offs are left-hand rest strokes, so the string is pulled down and against the adjacent string. When pulling off, be sure to relax the finger after the pull and let it bounce off the adjacent string. There are free-stroke pull-offs too, but they are less common.

- Strive for consistency in tone and volume between the different finger combinations.

- Because controlling the volume of slurs is always a challenge, try accenting the slurred note so it is louder than the articulated note. You'll find that the right and left hand have to work together to achieve this. You not only have to have good control over the slur in the left hand, but you must also be sensitive in the right hand about how hard you pluck the string.

STORT SLURS

C. Czerny
arr. David Patterson

14

STUDY 5: G Major

Once the basic two-note slur is mastered, it's time to move on to more complex techniques involving hammer-ons and pull-offs. This study incorporates mostly long slurs of three or more notes. Additionally, there are a few instances of what I call "ghost slurs." A "ghost slur" is a hammer-on or pull-off that is not preceded by an articulation on the same string (see footnote on following page). Executing these slurs with precision and good tone will take some work.

You will find it challenging to play this study evenly, and it will be especially difficult to articulate the notes such that the sixteenth-note groups sound like groups of four. You will have to proceed carefully and slowly when learning the piece. Your diligence will pay off well, however. You will notice a significant improvement in strength, flexibility, finger independence, and efficiency of motion.

PRACTICE TIPS:

- Try to feel the energy shift from finger to finger as you hammer or pull off. Don't keep pressure on fingers that are not playing.
- Be careful not to rush the groups of notes. Practice slowly enough where you have complete awareness and control over your fingers.
- Don't "pre-bend" notes when you do pull-offs. Only apply energy at the last moment, flicking the note off the string. Remember: you're simply plucking with the left hand.
- Use a metronome, and place the click on different parts of the beat to work on evenness.
- Listen for tone. Try to be consistent in tone and volume, and don't pluck too hard with the right hand.

LONG SLURS

C. Czerny
arr. David Patterson

Tuning:
(low to high) D-A-D-G-B-E

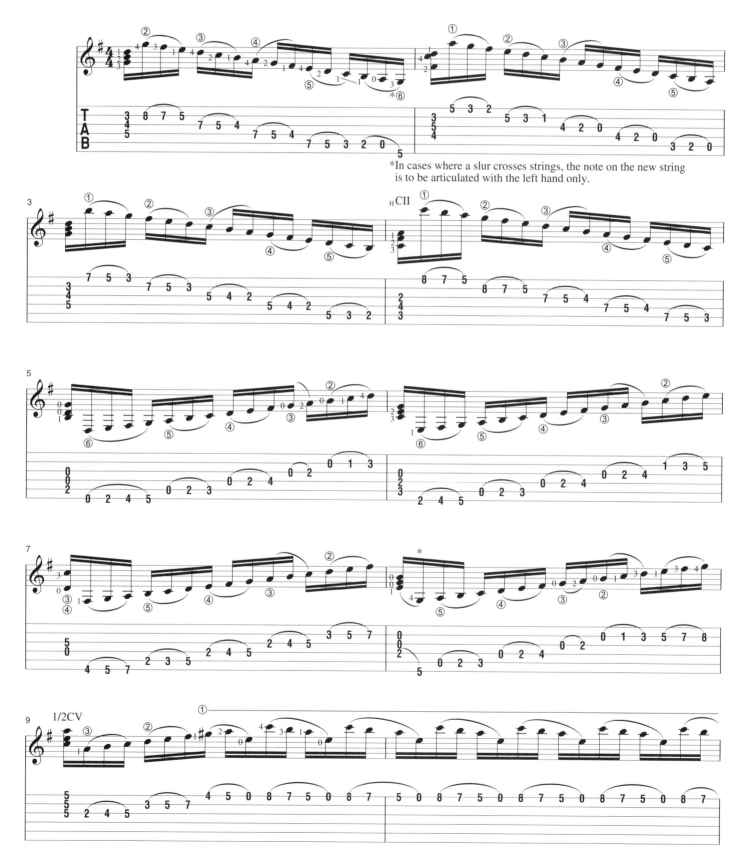

*In cases where a slur crosses strings, the note on the new string
 is to be articulated with the left hand only.

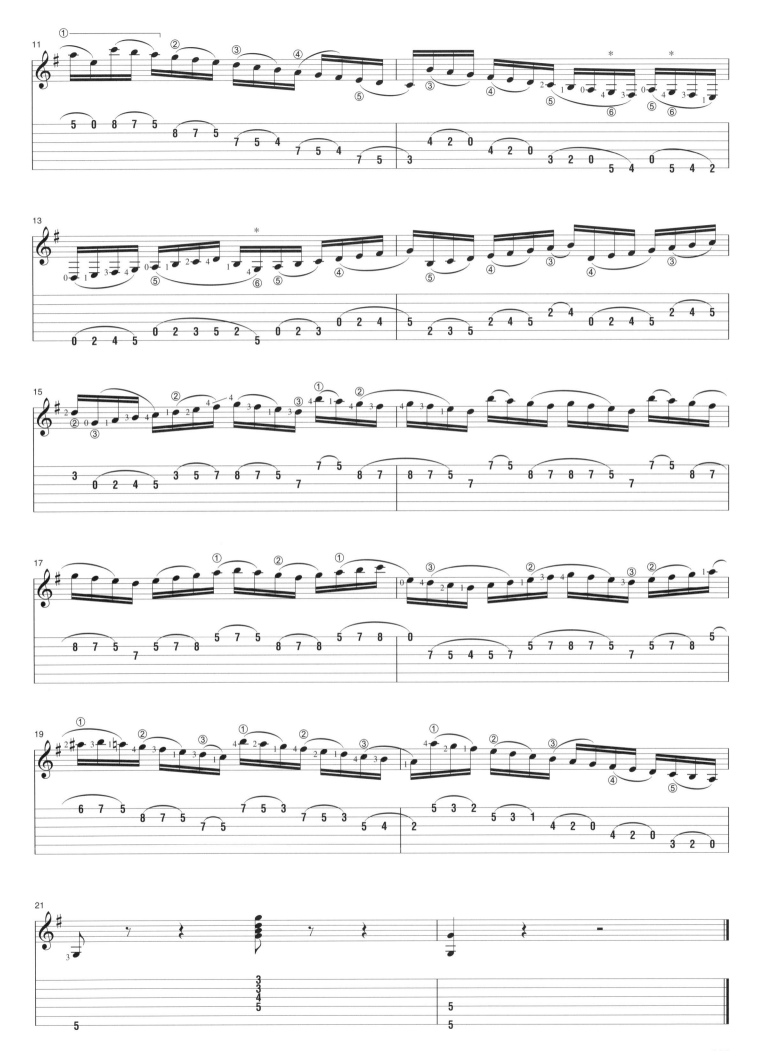

STUDY 6: D Major

Learning scales along the string horizontally can be a liberating experience. If you become familiar with each string horizontally, you will exponentially increase your understanding of the fingerboard. Your reading skills, ideas for fingering, and overall confidence moving around the fingerboard will improve greatly.

I intentionally did not finger the chords in the right hand as people have different preferences (p–i–m or i–m–a).

I hope you will have as much fun with this study as I have had. It truly represents an extreme when it comes to shifting—especially the second half!

PRACTICE TIPS:

- Keep your eyes ahead of your hands. If you choose to watch your left hand, let your eyes target the shifting points well ahead of your fingers. Eventually, try it without looking at the fingerboard. See if you can feel the shifts.

- The glissando section is quite difficult especially in measure 10. If playing the glissando from the E to the B on first string is too radical for you, feel free to re-finger the B on the second string with a two-string bar and play that passage in twelfth position.

- When working at a slow tempo, I have found it very useful to prepare the right hand finger prior to a shift.

- Don't rush the note prior to the shift. A good way of working on this is to play the study with dotted rhythms (both ways) or to play with it evenly with a metronome clicking on the last sixteenth note instead of the downbeat.

SHIFTING/GLISSANDO

C. Czerny
arr. David Patterson

*In meas. 9–12, where a slur/gliss connects two notes, the second note is not articulated.

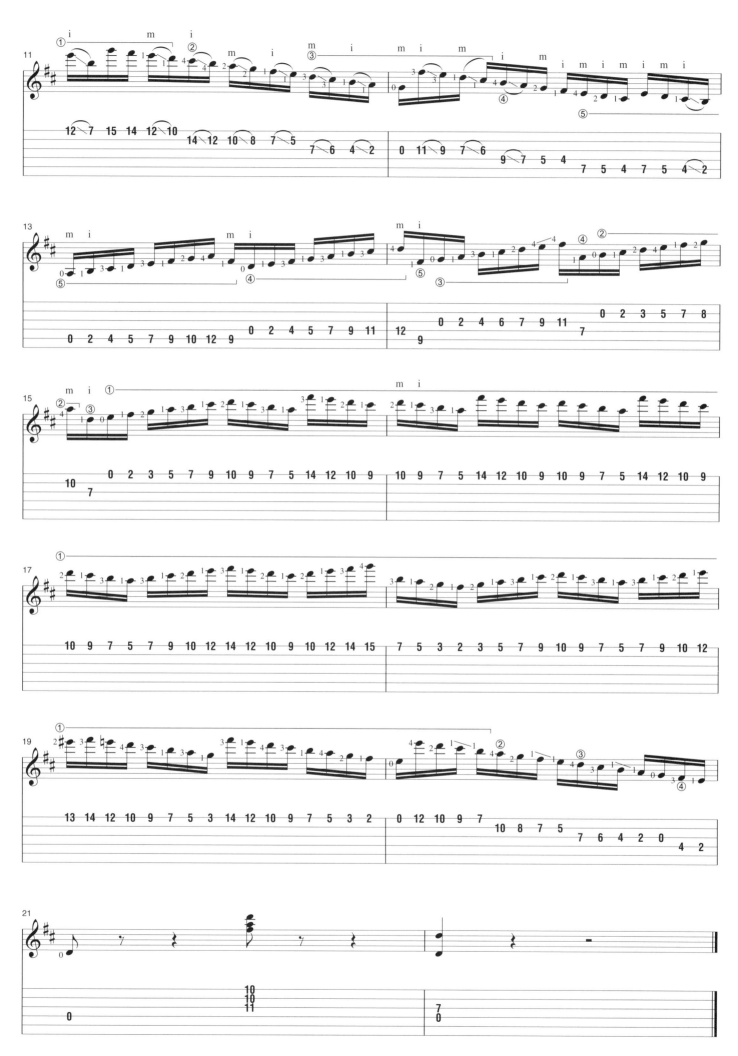

STUDY 7: A♭ Major

One of the most effective tools for working on challenging musical passages is the use of dotted rhythms. Using dotted rhythms reveals and/or highlights difficult points in a given passage by requiring the fingers to move twice as fast to accommodate a shift, string crossing, or jump to a chord.

When working on passages with duple rhythms (eighth and sixteenth notes), there are two rhythmic variations one can use:

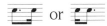 or

Usually, one will be more effective than the other in a particular passage depending on the nature of the music. You should always practice both and then focus on the more difficult of the two.

In this study, you will be required to tune the sixth string down to E♭ in order to accommodate the key. While this may seem a little unusual, it's quite easy to get used to.

PRACTICE TIPS:

- Make sure to play the dotted rhythms accurately. Do not "triplet-ize" or "swing" the thirty-second notes. Subdivide the beats using your voice or a metronome at first.

- Listen carefully to your accenting when playing the short, long variation. Be sure to accent the downbeat and not the second note. It's easy to turn the beat around when working on this rhythm.

- Work on this study using various right-hand fingerings, especially ones involving "a." Also try p–i and p–m.

DOTTED RHYTHMS

C. Czerny
arr. David Patterson

Tuning:
(low to high) E♭-A-D-G-B-E

STUDY 8: B Major

Practicing slowly is essential for building a strong foundation. We work slowly so that our physical habits are sound and so that every detail of what we are doing is clear in our hands, eyes, and ears. However, it is also important to incorporate speed into our practice by, well... playing fast. Speed bursts are a great way of getting the fingers moving quickly while maintaining control over the notes. Because the speed occurs in short bursts, one can better keep the hands in synch and focus on what is happening.

I used triplets and quintuplets in this study, but speed bursts can be comprised of as few as two notes (dotted rhythm for example) or several notes (an entire scale). Regardless of the number of notes in the burst, you should never play faster than you can play cleanly and with good tone. Speed is a relative matter and is developed over time. Keep in mind that speed is not just a matter of BPM. Controlling the rhythm, tone, and synchronization is equally if not more important than sheer finger velocity. It's OK to work at the edge of your ability, but once you cross the line where things sound sloppy and out of control, you are doing a disservice to yourself and the music!

PRACTICE TIPS:

- Try to learn this study right-hand only. It's worth the extra effort.
- Mute the strings by placing a folded cloth under them near the bridge and play the study without pitches. Think of yourself as a percussionist and concentrate on rhythmic accuracy.
- Watch those quintuplets! Make sure you play them evenly and don't rush.

SPEED BURSTS

C. Czerny
arr. David Patterson

*Right hand finger is repeated to begin new pattern.

STUDY 9: E♭ Major

While classical guitarists don't play in and beyond the twelfth position nearly as much as electric guitarists do, it is nonetheless an important area of study. Similarly to the shifting/glissando study, this arrangement represents an extreme challenge.

Because traditional classical guitars don't have cut-away bodies, playing in the upper range can be frustrating, requiring all sorts of hand, arm, and body contortions. Playing effectively beyond the twelfth fret is challenging enough, however it is often making the transition from a lower position where problems occur. The nice thing about this study is that, while it does stay in the upper range (beyond the twelfth fret) for extended periods of time, it also provides good practice in shifting from lower positions.

PRACTICE TIPS:

- This is one of those studies where I must caution you to be careful! Be aware of your hands and body. It will take some time to work out and develop the gymnastics here. Don't stress your wrist or fingers by over-practicing or repeating passages over and over. Take some time to think about the larger movements the body has to make. For example, you may have to dip your shoulder way down once you are up beyond twelfth position. That's OK, but be sure to correct your body when you return to a lower position. The same is true of the wrist. You will have to bring it out pretty far to reach those high notes, but find the point where you can return to the normal position. Don't keep the wrist extended when you don't have to.

- Mind where your right hand plucks along the string. As you play up in higher positions, you will have to move your right hand a bit farther towards the bridge in order to avoid playing on the nodal point of the string. The node is at the halfway point along the string where the octave harmonic is located. To demonstrate this, pluck an open string and, as you pluck it, slowly move your right hand towards the twelfth fret. You will notice the tone getting darker as you move to the left. When you reach the twelfth fret (the node), the sound is quite hollow. Now, if you fret a note, say a G at the third fret of the first string, you have shortened the string and moved the node (halfway point) to the fifteenth fret. Once you start fretting notes beyond the eighth and ninth frets, the nodal points begin to occur in the area where the right hand is plucking. If you don't compensate by shifting your right hand and staying to the right of the node, you will play on the node or even to the left of it. The notes will not speak as well and lack presence and richness of tone.

UPPER RANGE

C. Czerny
arr. David Patterson

STUDY 10: D♭ Major

The practice of arpeggios is vital to any instrument not only as a technical consideration but also as a way to work on your ears and understanding of harmony as it relates to the music you play. Pianists, string players, wind players, and vocalists in all genres of music practice arpeggios as a normal course of study, so it has always been a bit of a mystery to me why the practice of arpeggios has been somewhat neglected in the world of classical guitar. Perhaps you are scratching your head and saying, "What about the Giuliani 120 studies or the countless Sor and Carcassi studies dedicated to arpeggios?" Let me clarify. By arpeggio, I am not referring to fingering a chord shape and breaking it apart with a variety of right-hand patterns. I'm talking about playing a succession of chord tones in a linear fashion (root, 3rd, 5th, 7th) in a one to three octave range. I think the corresponding study will speak for itself. Try playing this study both rest and free stroke. I think you will find it to be very enjoyable as well as beneficial. You'll get plenty of exercise crossing strings in the right hand, while shifting and stretching in the left.

PRACTICE TIPS:

- Right-hand only practice is recommended once again! I know I've suggested it a lot in this book, but it is such a valuable tool for gaining security and awareness. It will be challenging to play right-hand only, so take your time.

- This study incorporates the use of shifts, stretching, and squeeze-shifts. It's easy to make mistakes at first, so always know ahead of time where you're going and how you're going to get there. Try to feel and see the shift or stretch in your mind before you start to move your hands.

- There's a lot of right-hand string crossing involved with this one. Keep your plucking fingers perpendicular to the strings and take care not to drift to the left or right.

ARPEGGIOS

C. Czerny
arr. David Patterson

STUDY 11: C Major

Playing scales using cross-string fingerings can produce a beautiful harp-like effect. It can also make difficult scale passages sound remarkably legato, fluid, and effortless. Working out cross-string scale fingerings is a little tricky at first, but with some practice, you will find it to be a useful and fun tool to have at your disposal.

In time, you will be able to control the amount of ringing from note to note as you cross strings—much in the same way a pianist would add more or less pedal to a passage. This is done primarily by the left hand and how long you choose to hold down certain notes.

Cross-string playing on the guitar tends to be key specific because the technique utilizes open strings whenever possible to facilitate fingering. The more open strings in the key, the easier it is to find cross-string scale patterns that work. Some good keys for exploring cross-string scale fingerings are: C major, A minor, F major, D minor, G major, E minor, D major, and A major. Once you start getting into multiple sharps and flats, options decrease significantly.

PRACTICE TIPS:

- This is an excellent study for focusing on right-hand only practice. Isolate sections and work on the right-hand fingering alone. You may find this to be very revealing and helpful when you go back and put the hands together.

- I fingered the thumb to play freely throughout this study, meaning that it may be used on both accented and non-accented beats. Listen carefully, and make an effort to control the volume and tone of the thumb so that it matches the volume and tone of the other fingers.

- Some passages in this study include slurs. Try to match the volume, evenness, and tone of the plucked notes and the slurred notes so that these passages sound seamless.

- This study requires many left-hand stretches, so if you're not used to that, be careful at first. Be physically aware, stay relaxed, and don't overdo it. If your left hand or wrist starts to feel sore, take a break, or practice the right hand only for a while. With time, your endurance will build.

CROSS-STRING/LEGATO

C. Czerny
arr. David Patterson

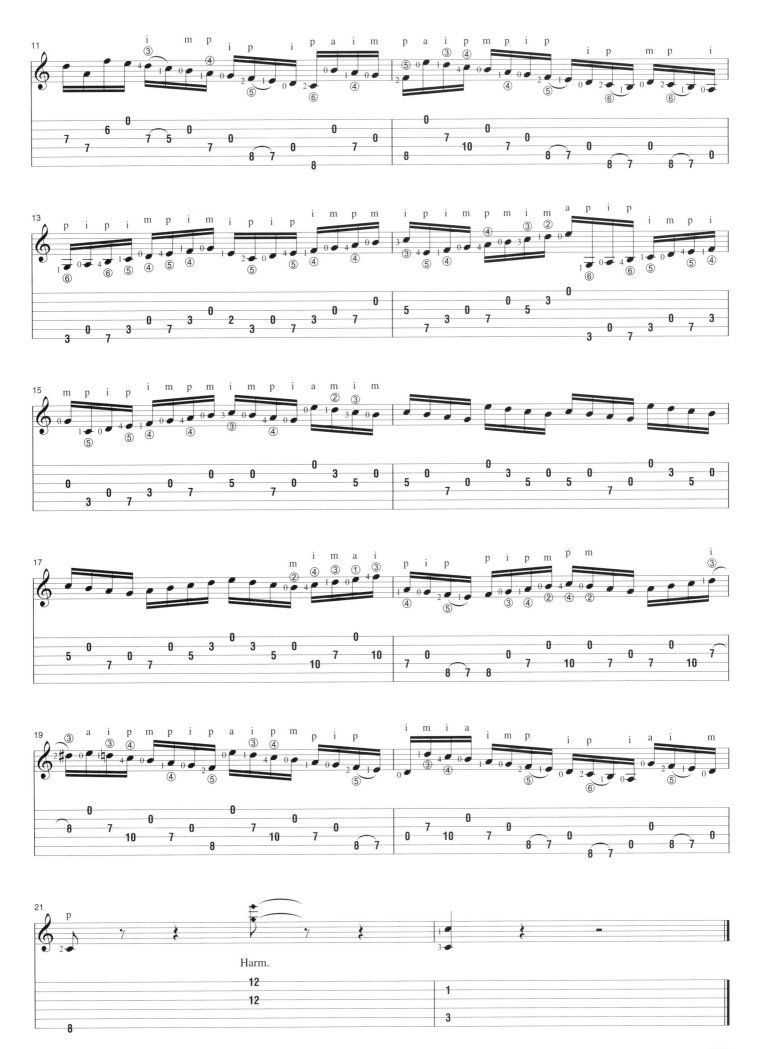

STUDY 12: E Major

This study, arranged in octaves, is one of the more difficult ones in the book but is also very rewarding as it yields many opportunities for development of both hands. For the left hand, the study is challenging both horizontally and vertically. Shifting smoothly along the strings while exchanging fingers will build your dexterity and strength. For the right hand, using various patterns such as tremolo and broken octaves with p–i or p–m will make working on the study more interesting and beneficial.

I want to say a few words about intonation, one of the many focal points of this octave study. The guitar encompasses aspects of both tempered and non-tempered instruments. Regardless of your individual philosophy on tuning or the method you choose to tune your guitar, the fact is that as guitarists we must constantly adjust intonation with the left hand. Since our hands are in direct contact with the strings, even if the guitar is tuned perfectly, the angle and pressure of the left hand fingers can push or pull the strings out of tune. Take note as you play this study how different hand shapes present different issues with intonation. Certain fingers want to push or pull a string flat or sharp. Some shapes play better in tune naturally than others. Work on adjusting the intonation in the more problematic shapes by pushing or pulling a certain finger more or less. It's intense work but well worth the effort. Working on intonation will sharpen up your ears significantly and over time will work its way into your overall playing.

PRACTICE TIPS:

Left Hand:

- If necessary, feel free to study only a few lines or even a few measures at a time. There's no need to take on the whole study at first. Avoid overworking your hand.

- Speed is the last thing on your to-do list with this one. Play it slowly, concentrating on details such as smooth shifting, intonation, and exchange of fingers. Speed will develop on its own over time (a long time).

- Keep an eye on your left wrist. Only bring it out as much as you need to accommodate certain shapes. Don't over extend it.

- To aid you in developing your ear, try working with a chromatic tuner. It can be helpful to have the visual support when you first begin this work. Play each note in the octave shape and see which one is out of tune. Then adjust it with your finger. Eventually, you will learn to adjust notes within a chord or key. Remember that one note can vary significantly in pitch depending on its function within a chord or key. For example, a B as the leading tone in the key of C is sharper than a B as the major third in the key of G.

- Be careful not to use too much pressure in the left hand. A lighter touch will help you conserve energy and will be better for intonation, shifting, and finger exchange.

- Playing the study as written with octaves played together is the most difficult for the left hand. Playing the study in broken octaves is a bit easier, so feel free to start working on it with some of the right hand suggestions below before attempting it as written.

Right Hand:

- Try some of these variations:

OCTAVES

C. Czerny
arr. David Patterson

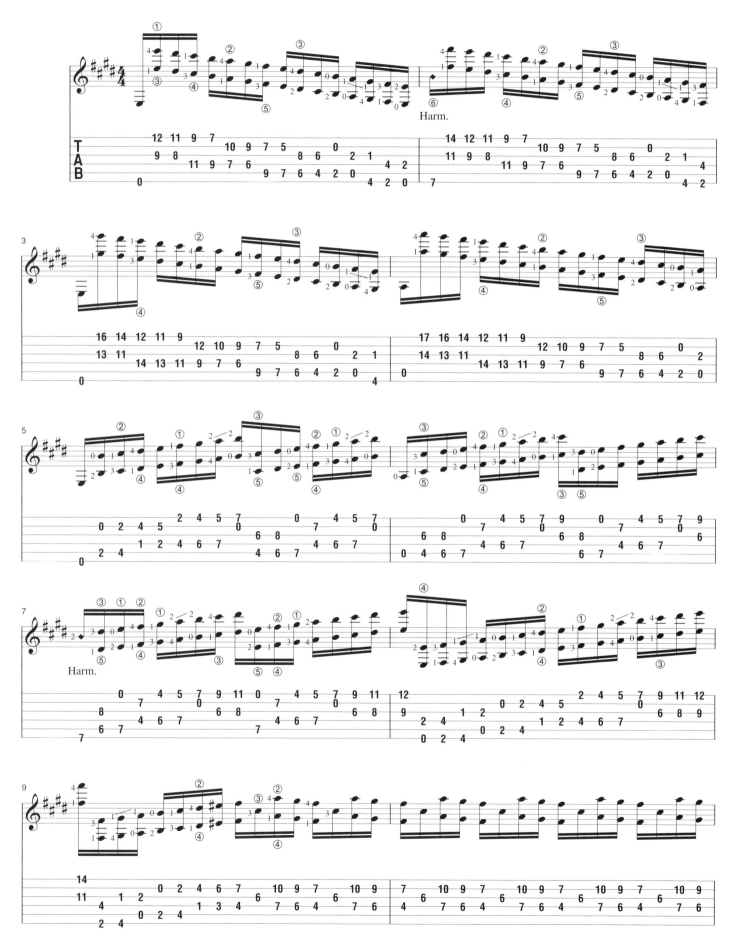

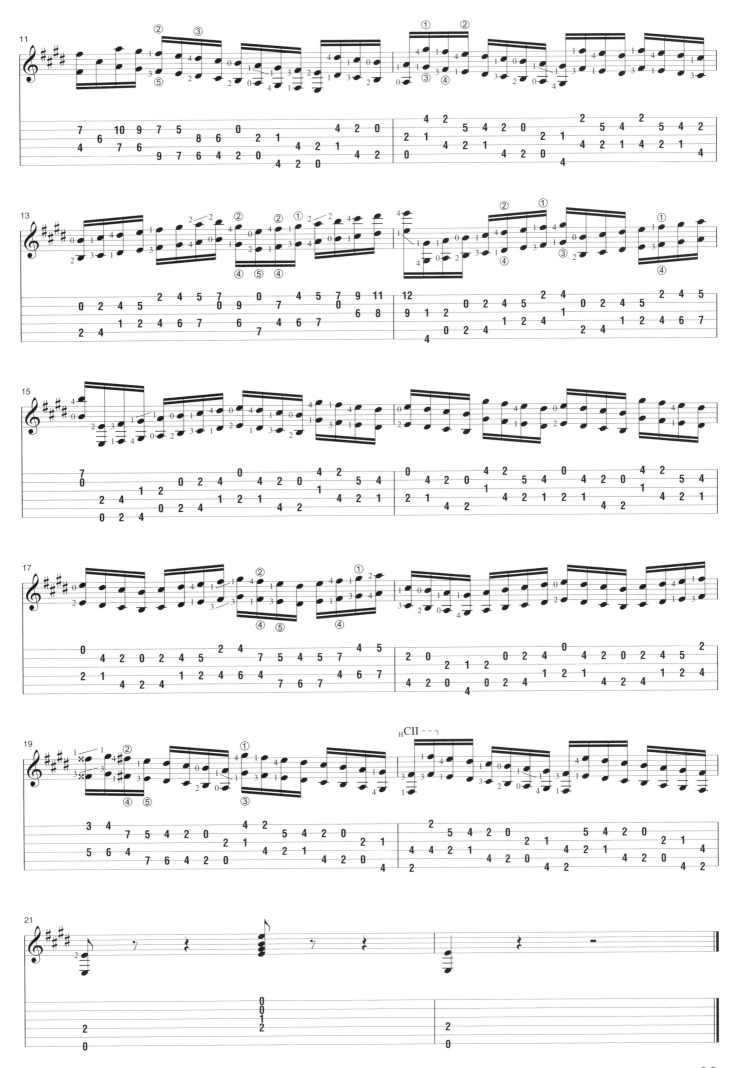

BIOGRAPHY

David Patterson is a guitarist and arranger. He has appeared as a soloist and chamber musician on stages worldwide as well as television and radio and has performed with various ensembles including the Auros Group, Musica Viva, The Boston Modern Orchestra Project, and the Harvard Group for New Music. David has been a guest artist at the Bowdoin and Tanglewood music festivals where, in 2003, he worked closely with composer Osvaldo Golijov and soprano Dawn Upshaw in the world premiere of the opera *Ainadamar*.

PHOTO BY M. CHEN

Patterson founded the critically acclaimed New World Guitar Trio and for fifteen years acted as the group's arranger and producer. The NWGT gained international recognition through its arrangements, commissions, recordings, and innovative performance style.

In 2003, David's recording of Jimmy Page's "White Summer/Black Mountainside" was featured in a compilation CD *Guitar Harvest* along with guitarists Andy Summers, Bill Frizel, and Ralph Towner, among others.

David is currently a faculty member at Tufts University, Longy Conservatory of Music, and Gordon College. He has conducted master classes internationally at various music institutions in the United States, South America, and Asia.

DEDICATION

I would like to thank my dear friends Jonathan Feist and Francis Perry for their help, support, and generosity over the course of developing this book.

This book is dedicated in memory of Charlie Banacos.